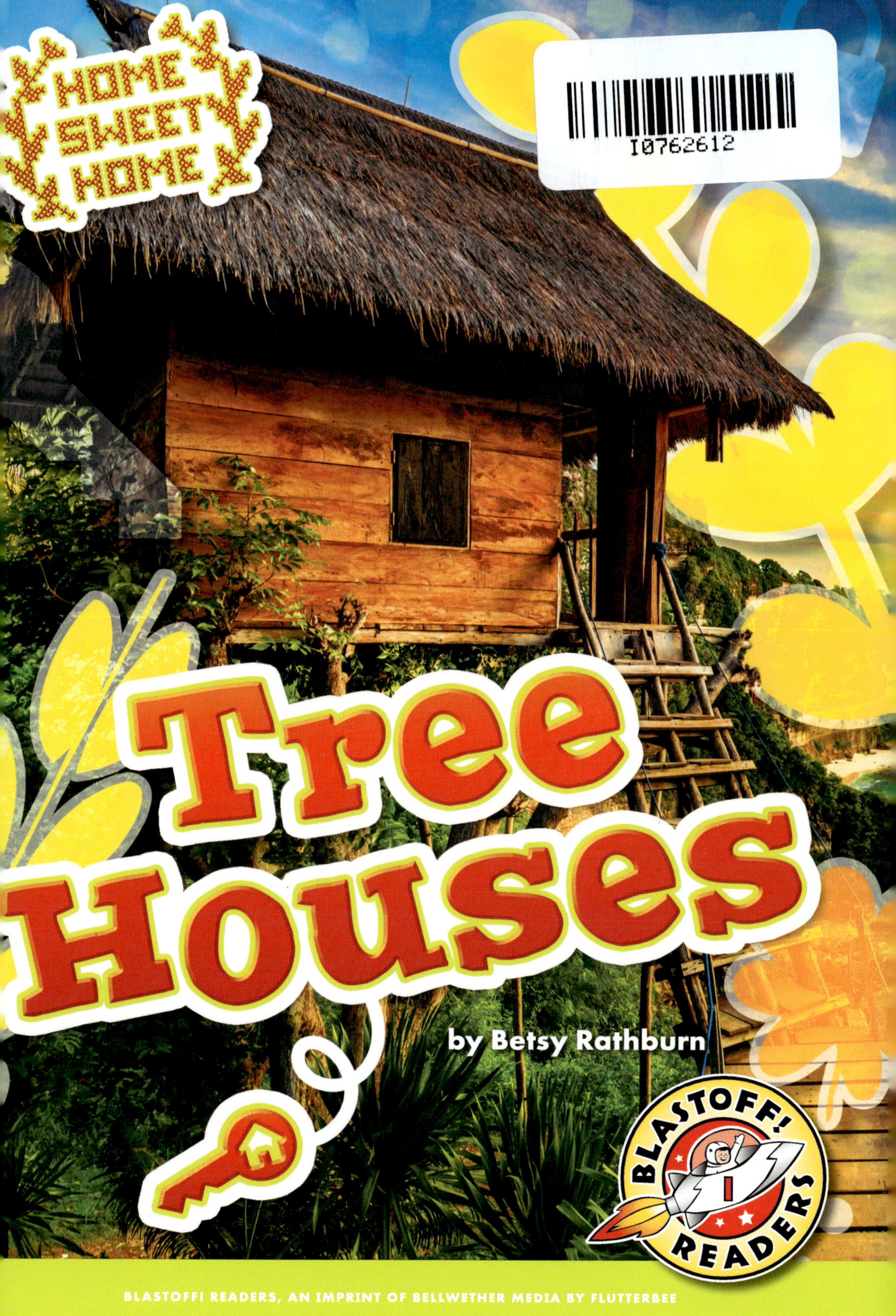
HOME SWEET HOME
Tree Houses
by Betsy Rathburn
BLASTOFF! READERS 1
BLASTOFF! READERS, AN IMPRINT OF BELLWETHER MEDIA BY FLUTTERBEE

Blastoff! Readers are carefully developed by literacy experts to build reading stamina and move students toward fluency by combining standards-based content with developmentally appropriate text.

Level 1 provides the most support through repetition of high-frequency words, light text, predictable sentence patterns, and strong visual support.

Level 2 offers early readers a bit more challenge through varied sentences, increased text load, and text-supportive special features.

Level 3 advances early-fluent readers toward fluency through increased text load, less reliance on photos, advancing concepts, longer sentences, and more complex special features.

★ **Blastoff! Universe**

Reading Level

Grade K

Grades 1–3

Grade 4

This edition first published in 2027 by Bellwether Media, Inc.

For information regarding permission, write to Bellwether Media, Inc., Attention: Permissions Department, 3500 American Blvd W, Suite 150, Bloomington, MN 55431.

Library of Congress Cataloging-in-Publication Data

Names: Rathburn, Betsy author
Title: Tree houses / by Betsy Rathburn.
Description: Minneapolis, Minnesota : Bellwether Media, Inc., [2026] | Series: Home sweet home | Includes bibliographical references and index. | Audience: Ages 5-8 | Audience: Grades 2-3 | Summary: "Developed by literacy experts for students in kindergarten through grade three, this book introduces tree houses to young readers through leveled text and related photos"– Provided by publisher.
Identifiers: LCCN 2026011846 (print) | LCCN 2026011847 (ebook) | ISBN 9798898800307 library binding | ISBN 9798898802837 paperback | ISBN 9798898801540 ebook
Subjects: LCSH: Tree houses
Classification: LCC TH4885 .R38 2026 (print) | LCC TH4885 (ebook)
LC record available at https://lccn.loc.gov/2026011846
LC ebook record available at https://lccn.loc.gov/2026011847

Editor: Rebecca Sabelko   Designer: Andrea Schneider

Printed in the United States of America, North Mankato, MN.

Table of Contents

Playhouse

We play on the tree swing. It is part of our tree house!

What Are Tree Houses?

Many tree houses are built high in trees. Some are on **stilts**.

stilts

Tree houses are often used for play. But some people live in them.

Most tree houses are small. Some are big. The biggest have more than one **story**!

stories
Size of a Tree House
garden with
64 tomato
plants
1 tree
house

Inside a Tree House

Stairs or **ladders** lead to the **porch**. A tree trunk may grow through the porch!

porch
tree trunk
ladder

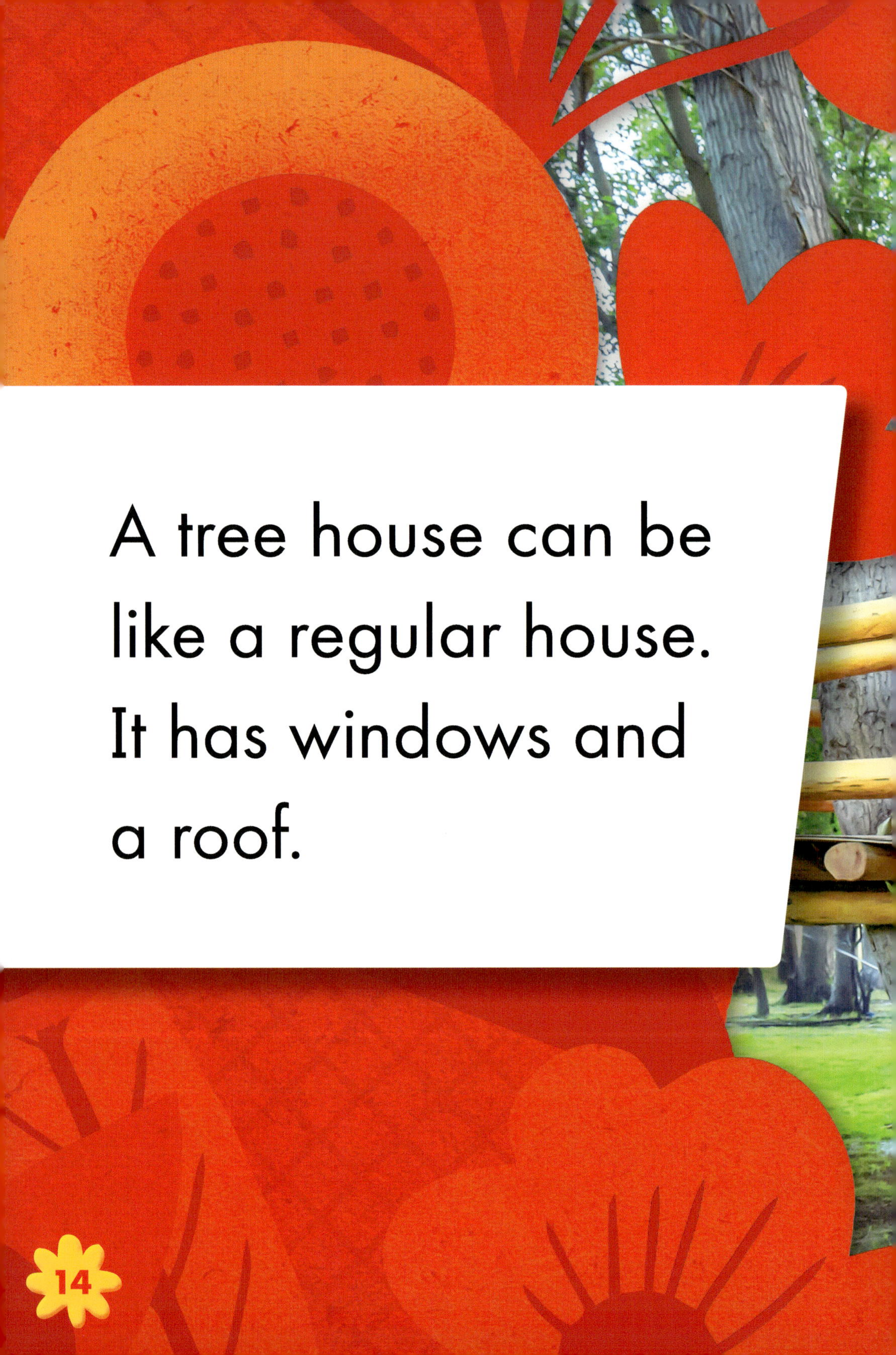

A tree house can be like a regular house. It has windows and a roof.

roof
windows

A tree house can have different rooms. **Furniture** must be lifted into place.

furniture

It may have a kitchen and a bathroom.

bathroom
kitchen

Some tree houses have **bridges** between trees. Tree houses are fun places to live and play!

bridge
Parts of a Tree House
porch
bridge
ladder

Glossary

bridges

walkways that connect two places

furniture

items such as chairs and tables that make rooms ready to use

ladders

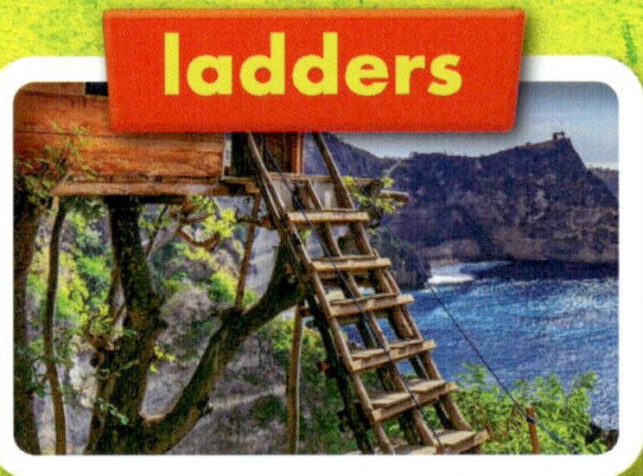

things used to climb

porch

an area outside the front entrance of a home

stilts

tall poles that hold a house above the ground

story

a floor in a building

To Learn More

AT THE LIBRARY

Lawrence, Ellen. *Homes Around the World*. Minneapolis, Minn.: Ruby Tuesday Books, 2025.

Jones, Christianne. *Measuring at Home*. North Mankato, Minn.: Pebble, 2022.

Rathburn, Betsy. *Houseboats*. Minneapolis, Minn.: Bellwether Media, 2027.

ON THE WEB

FACTSURFER

Factsurfer.com gives you a safe, fun way to find more information.

1. Go to www.factsurfer.com.
2. Enter "tree houses" into the search box and click 🔍.
3. Select your book cover to see a list of related content.

Index

The images in this book are reproduced through the courtesy of: Helminadia/ Getty Images, front cover; Lan, p. 3 (ladder); Sarawut, p. 3 (trees); Passakorn, p. 3 (bird); nok6716, pp. 4-5; Seba Rem/ Getty Images, pp. 6-7; Kattiyaearn, p. 7 (stilts); wundervisuals/ Getty Images, pp. 8-9; Nicolle, pp. 10-11, 22 (story); Sanzida Habib, pp. 12-13; Cristian Martin/ Getty Images, pp. 14-15, 22 (porch); fokkebok/ Getty Images, pp. 16-17; SrdjanPav, p. 17 (furniture); Mint Images Limited/ Alamy, pp. 18-19; picture alliance/ Getty Images, p. 19 (bathroom); fottoo, pp. 20-21; Dayalguru, p. 21 (parts); Dolierya, p. 21 (bridge); lokeshkumar, p. 22 (bridges); MelanieMaya/ Getty Images, p. 22 (furniture); tawatchai1990, p. 22 (ladders); Athulvis/ Wikicommons, p. 22 (silts).